THE RACING RETIREMENT PLAN

How to Systematically Increase Your Wealth from Horserace Betting

By
Bernard Hibbert

ISBN 0-9546205-2-6

Copyright: Bernard Hibbert 2004

Published by
SPORTSWORLD PUBLISHING LTD.
Raines House, Denby Dale Road, Wakefield WF1 1HL
www.sportsworldpublishing.co.uk

CONTENTS

Part One

THE BACKGROUND

Part Two

THE RACING INVESTMENT PROGRAMME

Systems

FOREWORD

The Psychology of Betting

The correct mental attitude is essential to make a success of this business. To be a winner you have to think like a winner. Sounds like pretty obvious 'positive thinking' stuff - but it really does work! Tell yourself you are a professional backer of racehorses. <u>Visualise</u> the lifestyle. You are retired or semi-retired from mundane occupations and now make the bulk of your income from your newly chosen profession. You are serious about your work but are now able to enjoy extended leisure time to do the things you never got around to. You are keen and enthusiastic. When you wake up in the morning you can't wait to get stuck in to the day's business. You're all done by 9:00am and ready to strike any bets as soon as the bookmakers' offices open. Then you're finished for the day - unless you decide to watch the day's sport and follow the live betting on television. Or maybe you have planned a day on-course at your local track. It could be a winning day. It could be a losing day. No matter. You know your strategies will show your required profit in the long term. Life is fun!

If you visualise how it will be it <u>can</u> become reality. Believe me, as long as your desires (and they must be burning desires) are actually attainable, you can make them happen. If you are constantly telling your sub-conscious what you want, the amazing mechanism in your brain *will find a way to make it so*.

You will make mistakes along the way but don't be deterred.
Start with small stakes. That way the odd blunder will sting but not devastate.

If you think you're beaten, you are,
If you think you dare not, you don't.
If you like to win, but think you can't,
It is almost certain you won't.

If you think you'll lose, you're lost.
For out of the world we find,
Success begins with a fellow's will -
It's all in the state of mind.

If you think you're outclassed, you are.
You've got to think high to rise.
You've got to be sure of yourself before
You can ever win that prize.

Life's battles don't always go
To the stronger or faster man.
But soon or late the man who wins
Is the man WHO THINKS HE CAN!

THE RACING RETIREMENT PLAN

Part One ~ The Background

INTRODUCTION

"The man who wins is the one who walks away with a profit". Terry Ramsden. 1987

Why do we bet?
Well, there is no doubt it can be exciting fun, but we all know the real reason is the allure of easy money! Unfortunately we must stop right there and examine some cold hard facts.

The reason most bookmakers flourish is because no more than 10% of punters make a regular profit from the game. The other 90% lose an average of 20p in the pound overall. So, who are these elite 10% and how do they do it?

We have to remember that the bookmaker is a *professional*. All his time, energy and resources are directed towards his business. Also, we are essentially playing his game because he sets the odds and can manipulate them during play. So how can we possibly win? Well, it is not easy - but not quite as difficult as many people imagine.

Remember that the punter does have one significant advantage - he can be *selective*. The bookmaker is obliged to bet on every race but we can wait for the right opportunity when things are in our favour. The most important thing is to *think like a winner* and adopt a professional attitude. We have to be prepared to put in the necessary time and work to reap the rewards.

An orderly and disciplined approach is essential and we will discuss the merits of keeping records, correct staking with an adequate betting bank and so on.

It is only in the last few years that I have discovered a way to make a regular profit from betting on racehorses, but I would never rely on it for a living - much too stressful. Being semi-retired I have a basic income that pays the bills and my betting profits provide the 'jam'. It is advisable not to be greedy. Try to place too many large (winning) bets and you will have difficulty 'getting on', particularly with smaller bookmakers with limited turnovers. (Having said that I have been 'knocked back' by Ladbrokes before now!) Spread your bets around with several different bookmakers, moving on after a good win. You should also explore the opportunities now available on the Betting Exchanges where we can set our own odds and bet directly with other punters.

Remember that all my methods require some personal judgement in their operation. Blindly following rigid rules, with no consideration of other factors, will not do. So, if there is a sudden change in the going conditions that will not suit our system horse, or our selection is badly drawn in a race where a good draw is all-important - NO BET. I Recommend you do a dry run on paper for at least a month before placing bets on any system to gain confidence.

The object of this book is to make you money. It's as simple as that. Therefore, it will contain no waffle and only the occasional trivial anecdote! It will explain how you can make serious money right now. And how you can continue to do so for as long as you wish.

Don't listen to people who tell you that the only winner is the bookmaker. Yes, it's true that the majority of punters lose. But, set about this business in a systematic way and it's so easy to become a winner. And now that betting duty is a thing of the past your income is also tax-free!
Unlike most other books on this subject I will tell you exactly how to set up your betting strategy and give you methods that all have at least three years checkable results, proving to you that these systems really work.

I have read just about every publication on horseracing and I can tell you that this book is unique. It will unlock the secrets of *systematically increasing your wealth* clearly and concisely. No theories or ambiguity, just cold hard facts that cannot be disputed.

Now, before we start, tell me, having read this introduction, aren't you glad that you bought this book?

Right, let's make a start and see if we can't join the 10% club!

From now on we will be thinking like *investors* not gamblers.

CHAPTER ONE

Money in the Bank

"To beat the bookies you must work at it, then work some more and keep on working. I've been going racing for twenty years and I'm still learning. But the bookies can be beaten". Julian Wilson. 1974

The great thing about our business is that you can have a great deal of fun while you're making money - so let's get this chapter quickly out of the way.

Every new conventional business has to contend with the 'boring bits' before it starts to trade. You need to see an accountant, inform the Inland Revenue, register with Customs & Excise for VAT and so on. *In our business we need do none of these things*. However, before we get to the exciting part, it is absolutely essential that we set up our Betting Bank. I am, hopefully, preaching to the converted here, but without a betting bank you will surely fail.

Here's the reason. You know that you have a proven selection method that has given, say, a 40% winning strike rate at good enough prices to show a nice profit over the last three years. But, of course, this means that 60% of your selections will fail so you will have inevitable losing runs. Without an adequate bank, set aside for the sole purpose of betting, you will definitely 'bottle out' if you hit a double-figure losing run, which is always a possibility. You stop betting - and the bookmaker has won! Bookies have losing periods as well but they have resources to cover this and, operating their business in a sound and consistent way, make a profit in the long term.

So, let's examine how losing runs can affect you. The following probability chart will give you an approximate idea of the losing runs to expect, depending on your system's expected strike rate.

Longest Losing Run to Expect

Strike Rate	10% chance	5% chance	1% chance
25%	9	11	17
30%	7	9	13
35%	6	7	11
40%	5	6	10
45%	4	6	8
50%	4	5	7
60%	3	4	6

So, we see that, even with an excellent strike rate of 40%, it is quite possible to hit 10 losers on the run before we find another winner. The first essential then is to set up a working betting bank, then losers don't trouble you.

The accepted professional way to bet is to set up a bank of twenty points for each method you follow. This would be £200 if you start off with £10 units. Betting one point on each selection means your first bet is 5% of your bank. As your bank increases *continue betting 5% units*. In other words, if your bank increases to £250 your stake is now £12.50. When you reach £300 up your stake to £15 and so on. Continue to increase stakes in this way until you reach your maximum 'comfort zone' level. For example, if you feel that £100 would be the most you wish to wager - freeze your bank at that level and you can now feel free to cream off the profits.

Should you lose a few bets at first and your bank decreases to £150 lower your stakes to £7.50. If your selection method is sound it is impossible to imagine going broke using this plan.

One basic requirement you will need is a copy of the Racing Post every day. This is a necessary expense that will provide you with all the information you need to operate my systems. Personally, I do not spend several hours a day studying the formbooks. Much of this work is done for you by the experts in the racing press, providing you with statistics on just about everything. These days I simply spend an hour or two with my Racing Post early morning and find my various systems provide me with enough winners to turn a decent profit.

Maintaining detailed records of all your bets is extremely important to the long-term success of your operation. Of course, this is a pleasure when you're winning but becomes a chore when you're not! Nevertheless, it is essential for analysing weaknesses in your strategy and weeding out mistakes. Keep a loose-leaf file with full details of all bets struck.

Remember:
You are a *professional* operating a business. You need to know the profit/loss situation. Keep your books up to date.

CHAPTER TWO

Do systems work?

The short answer is yes, providing the criteria are based on sound logical principles and results checked over a lengthy period. I have followed systems for many years and believe that all professionals follow a *systematic* approach, although not necessarily blindly following a set of rules. We will discuss selectivity in the next chapter and how you can improve profits but first let's have a look at some basic ideas that are often used as a starting point to enhance a system's performance.

The Betting Forecast
It is a well-known fact that around 67% of all winners come from the first three in the betting. The first, second or third favourite win the majority of races. Bookmakers and odds compilers are perfectly aware of a horse's true chances and build this into the price accordingly. Market leaders, therefore, are one way of ensuring that your selections are among the potential winners.

The Forecast Price
Short priced favourites do not usually make for a really successful method. Betting at less than 2/1 means you are simply turning money over most of the time, with no real gain. Double figure outsiders are very nice if you can find them but very difficult to predict on a regular basis. Most successful systems tend to find selections

at an average price of 4/1. If you can couple this with a 30% strike rate you're definitely in the money with a 50% return on investment. (For every one hundred bets thirty win so the return is one hundred and twenty points. Take off the seventy losing bets and you make fifty points).

Handicaps or Non-Handicaps
Non-handicaps are easier to predict - around 40% of favourites win these races. However bookmakers are quite aware of this and prices are usually depressed. Only around 25% of favourites win handicap races but prices are much better so many successful systems are based on these races and can give a better profit in the long term. If you can formulate a method that embraces handicaps, with a 30% strike rate, you will most likely come out on top.

Is Your Selection Fit?
If, like most of us, you bet mainly off-course, there is no way of knowing for sure if your selection is fully wound-up for today's race - unless you happen to be a good friend of the trainer. A good *recent* run, however, can give us an indication of the horse's well-being. Many good systems, therefore, include a rule that the horse must have run within *thirty days or often less*. If the animal did not disgrace itself on that occasion we can presume that it will be reasonably fit today. Another point worth mentioning is that the more consistent animals tend to be *younger male horses*, particularly on the Flat.

Is the Horse in Form?

If your selection ran well last time, either winning or finishing in the money, there is every chance that it will repeat that good performance today. You know that both horse and stable are in form, especially if that last run was quite recent. Of course, many horses do win after a long losing run - going in today following an apparently poor performance last time - but these winners are almost impossible to predict under normal circumstances. So first, second or third last time out will always find winners.

Course & Distance Winners

Confidence is always boosted if your system selection has previously won at the course. It proves the horse is happy there and that the trainer knows what's required to produce winners. If the horse has already won over the same distance this eliminates any doubts about it getting the trip, particularly on the Flat. So, introducing a rule that the horse must have **CD** (or at least **D**) after its name can only help rather than hinder a system's effectiveness.

Trainers & Jockeys

If your horse is trained by one of the top stables at the track and/or ridden by one of the top jockeys, with a high winning strike rate, this can only strengthen its chances of going in today, particularly if it is a well-fancied market leader.

Race Runners

There is no doubt that most systems can be enhanced by reducing the number of runners in the races you are using. Restricting your choice to races that have between five and twelve runners, and certainly a maximum of sixteen will always tighten that strike rate. Stating the obvious, your horse has fewer rivals to beat and is less likely to encounter traffic problems.

Expert Opinion

Many decent systems are based on selections from newspaper correspondents. Following your favourite tipster blindly is highly unlikely to yield a profit but building expert opinion into your method can be a good idea. Horses that are top rated in your daily newspaper find their way into a lot of systems, as do the 'naps' or daily best bets from the top tipsters. Racing Post experts *Topspeed, Postmark, Postdata* & *Spotlight* are always worthy of consideration.

CHAPTER THREE

Selectivity is the Key

One of the criticisms aimed at system betting is that it can result in blindly following a set of rules that may not take into account changing circumstances on the day. For example, today's selection may have to beat a very strong odds-on favourite that, all things being equal, really shouldn't lose. Perhaps it has to overcome an unfavourable draw or run on going conditions not previously encountered. Today's race may be a hotly contested thirty runner handicap with several leading contenders and the price on offer does not represent true value and so on. Many of these points can be written into a system but there is no doubt that selectivity based on personal judgment is the key to enhancing that strike rate. I have checked out several good proven systems and attempted to exercise my own opinion as to whether the selection really is likely to win - with surprisingly good results. My records show that, after listing selections and then examining each race one by one, I was able to sift out horses with serious question marks and improve the strike rate by as much as 10%. Occasionally, I have to admit to getting it wrong. I eliminated a selection from calculations and it won anyway - very annoying! However, over a period, the odd missed winner was easily forgotten as many more losers were erased. All this is easier said than done of course but, if you have a favourite system, I suggest you list selections and then take each race apart and *form your own opinion* about the horse's true chances. Put a question mark by any you are unsure about. Check results at the end of the day and see if you were right or wrong. Like me, you may surprise yourself. So, what do we base these opinions on?

The Going
Sudden changes in underfoot conditions are probably one of the main causes of bad bets. If the previous form clearly shows that your selected horse has always run below par when the going is soft, a sudden downpour on the day should cause us to think twice. Inevitably, things are not always so cut and dried and you may find a strong selection, perhaps a younger horse with experience of only firm conditions, running today on 'good to soft'. We are now in the area of guesswork. How can we know if the horse will handle the ground unless we happen to know the trainer - and even he may not be sure! The answer here is *value*. If the price on offer compensates for your uncertainty it's probably still a reasonable bet. Finally, it is usually a good idea to suspend betting activities altogether in *extreme* conditions described as 'heavy' or 'hard'.

The Distance
Similar comments apply to the race distance. It obviously helps if the horse is proven over today's trip, either winning or finishing well, particularly at specialist distances like seven furlongs. If the horse is going into totally unknown territory - perhaps being tried over one mile after previously only running in sprints - a 'watching brief' with no bet is the best advice.

The Draw

Chester is famous for its almost circular track. Horses are on the turn nearly all the way round. Because of this it is extremely difficult for a horse to win a sprint race of five or six furlongs unless it has a low draw close to the rail. Anything drawn higher than stall five might as well stay at home unless the animal is *very* smart and has a top experienced jockey.

Look at these figures that I compiled over several seasons a few years ago.

CHESTER Winning draw positions, five furlongs:

Draw	Win %
1	21
2	16
3	15
4	20
5	11
TOTAL	83%

Because of Chester's tight turning track, horses drawn wider than five hardly ever win!

The same sort of draw bias operates at BEVERLEY in five furlong sprints only *the other way round*. At this track the **highest** five drawn win over 77% of the time. Obviously a good start from the gate is essential in sprints so make sure your horse does not have a record of being slowly away.

There are several other Flat courses with a strong draw bias and it really pays to be aware of this and judge the chances of your selection accordingly. You will find full details of any draw bias for each meeting in the *Racing Post's* 'TOPDRAW' box. Nothing is 'written in stone' however and some horses do overcome a bad draw and go on to win. I know this to my chagrin from a pleasant summer evening's racing at Chester's *Roodee* last year. I had abandoned my plans to lump on my strong system selection when I discovered it was drawn ten out of twelve runners. Anyway, no-one had told the horse that it couldn't win as it came around the outside on the final bend, going like a train, and just got up on the line in a photograph. My reaction and the expletives that followed are best not printed here!

Racecourse map of Chester

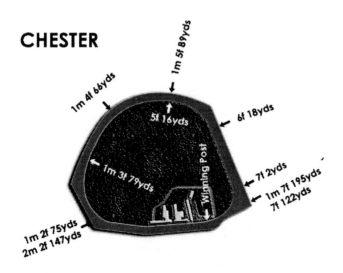

The Course Specialist

'Horses for Courses' is an old saying but how very, very true! The following tracks are those where a *previous course winner* is at a <u>distinct</u> advantage because of the particular peculiarities of the course.

Flat:

Ascot	Goodwood
Beverley	Lingfield
Brighton	Newcastle
Carlisle	Pontefract
Catterick	Southwell
Chester	Wolverhampton
Epsom	

National Hunt:

Aintree	Hexham
Ascot	Kelso
Carlisle	Leicester
Catterick	Lingfield
Cheltenham	Newcastle
Fakenham	Plumpton
Fontwell	Sandown
Haydock	Towcester

So, if your selection is running at any of these courses, having won there previously, this can only give you added confidence. If the horse has *never run at the course before* you would have some cause for concern and may decide not to bet, particularly if there are any other doubts.

Weight
There is a well-known saying in racing that is worth noting:
"Taking weight off poor horses won't make them run any faster. Putting more weight onto a good horse will eventually slow it down".

Handicapping is a very complicated subject so, unless you particularly want to make a study of it, my advice would be to ignore it. In most cases you can rely on the experts to point you in the right direction. If a horse is carrying too much weight, and therefore unlikely to win, the clues are usually obvious in the RP ratings, Spotlight comments and the price quoted.

RP ratings are the work of the Racing Post's private handicapper. His ratings are found on the right hand side of the race card underneath the allotted weight. The horse with the highest rating is the one he considers to be the best handicapped horse in the race. So, if your horse is among the top three or four rated you can be sure it is fairly handicapped on its past performances. It is always worth consulting the feature *'Ahead of the Handicapper'* in the **'Signposts'** pages of the Racing Post. Every day you will find a goldmine of good information and statistics packed into these pages on just about everything so they are well worth consulting.

The top weighted horse in a handicap is considered by the Official Handicapper to be the best animal in the race. Unfortunately a lot of them don't win! However, if we consider well-fancied runners at certain courses a good strike rate can be achieved. Research over four years revealed that the top weight in a handicap seemed to perform better than average at the following tracks *especially when it won its last race and is the forecast favourite today*.

Flat Racing:

Doncaster	Newmarket (Rowley)
Hamilton	Redcar
Haydock	Southwell
Lingfield (aw)	Yarmouth
Newcastle	

National Hunt Racing:

<u>Hurdles</u>:

Chepstow	Plumpton
Folkestone	Towcester
Hereford	Uttoxeter
Newbury	Wetherby

<u>Chases</u>:

Kempton	Wincanton
Musselburgh	Worcester
Newcastle	

Top weighted favourites that won their last race showed a level stake profit at all these courses from above average strike rates.

Speed

All things being equal, the fastest horse should win the race. Unfortunately, in horse racing, things are rarely equal!

Many races on turf are not 'truly run' particularly over longer distances. If a slow pace is set early on the race can develop into a tactical affair with jockeys playing a 'cat and mouse' game.

In American racing things are quite different. Firstly the majority of races are run on dirt - similar to our All-Weather tracks. Secondly, they tend to favour the shorter distance sprints and have fewer 'routes'. Also, most importantly, tracks in America have *sectional timing* where form is recorded with accurate timing for each furlong. As a result, many horseracing systems in the States use *pace and timing* to good effect.

At present I tend to disregard the clock for a lot of U.K. racing with the exception of sprints - particularly on All-Weather tracks. In these races the excellent *Topspeed*, of the Racing Post, comes into his own. It is well worth your while consulting the Topspeed ratings for all races, especially in the more truly-run sprints, and taking encouragement if your fancy is among the top rated.

British All-Weather racecourses have started to experiment with sectional timing and, when it becomes

established, will open the door for brand new systems involving speed ratings.
Watch this space!

Value
Enough has been written on this subject to fill several volumes but there is no denying it is the final key to profitable betting. I once heard *Derek Thompson* remark on Channel 4's Morning Line "*Value - the most expensive word in racing!*" and of course it can be if big prices are your only criteria. However, if you have a sound selection method used with the principle of value you must come out on top.

My own personal concept of value is this. I am not interested in short priced favourites at less than 2/1. I am even less interested in trying to find the 33/1 outsider that might go in occasionally. My preferred betting range is between 2/1 and 8/1, usually the first, second or third favourite. Good chance horses at a reasonable price will make you a very nice profit if your method finds you 30% winners at average odds of 4/1. So, if my selection is quoted in the betting forecast at, say, 4/1 I am perfectly happy if I can take a price of 5/1 or even 9/2 *providing* it fits the following rule.

If I decide that, all things being equal, there are really only four real contenders in the race from which the winner should come (and my selection is one of them) this means I have three other runners to beat. If we presume for a moment that these four contenders, in an ideal world, have roughly equal chances they should all be 3/1. I then add another point to cover the 'unknown' factor. Therefore, if I can get better than 4/1 I am perfectly satisfied. It's a little simplistic and not exactly 'A' level mathematics, but it works OK for me!

One final word about value. Always take an *early price* if you can. You will beat Starting Prices most of the time.

So, make your system selection and then look at as many aspects as you can including suitable going, distance, draw, handicap ratings, trainer currently in form and so on.

If there are two or more minus points against your horse you may wish to think again. If in doubt - leave it out.

Two or more <u>plus</u> points together with a <u>value price</u> and it begins to look like a worthy contender for your money.

Learn to make your own decisions based on the facts and forget about 'inside information' that can often be suspect. Bookmaker William Hill once wrote "Believe 95% of what you see and 5% of what you hear. And that's very doubtful, that 5%".

CHAPTER FOUR

Paddock Watching - Selectivity at the Racecourse

Did you know that on-course bookmakers' profit margins are *much* lower than their high street betting shop counterparts. The reasons are pretty obvious - the high level of competition in the betting ring plus the fact that they do not have the time to calculate the exotic multiple bets that are so profitable to off-course bookmakers. Unless you go racing regularly, the third reason may not be quite so obvious - but it is a very important factor. At the racetrack, customers have access to valuable information denied to the off-course punter. Racecourse punters get the chance to see exactly what they are betting on! Providing you know what to look for, many bad bets can be saved by observing your selection in the parade ring. Betting off-course you can't see that the horse looks like a loser today - all you have to go on is the formbook. If, like me, you like to bet on-course whenever possible, here are a few pointers I have learned that can improve your results dramatically. If a horse's appearance or body language fits one or more of these profiles you can have a pretty good idea of how it will run.

The Angry Horse
Watch out for any of these negative signs - ears flat back against the head - eyes take on a fixed glare - does not co-operate with handlers - thrashes head - swishes tail violently - could lash out with hind legs -

jockey wary of mounting. The horse will almost certainly lose.

The Frightened Horse
Carries head high in rapid motion - eyes roll violently - nostrils flared - ears constantly flicking in all directions.

Leg action is high and erratic - starts to sweat profusely. Reacts strongly to any noise or sudden movement and may shy from the crowd. Could resist being mounted and pulls very hard going down to the start, covered in sweat when it arrives and often gives trouble in the starting stalls. The horse will almost certainly lose.

The Green Horse
Carries its head rather high - looks around with curiosity, its ears constantly turning, showing its unfamiliarity with the racecourse. The horse may whinny and wheel about when the jockey tries to mount but, unlike angry or frightened horses, will accept the rider once they are aboard. Green horses can win but are not usually a good bet.

The Hurting Horse
Could well display the same signs as the frightened horse - it's scared because it knows racing will add to the pain. Bad signs are gnarled, knobbly knees and forelegs, front leg bandages and the smell of horse liniment. Going down to the start it will adopt a short bumpy stride because its arthritic front legs hurt when they touch the ground. The horse should not be running and will almost always lose.

The Dull Horse

Walks in a flat-footed manner with no spring in its step. Its coat is dull and displays no sheen. The head carriage is low with no arch to the neck and the ears may be sideways, pointing downward. Not in top condition, but can still win.

The Unfit Horse

This horse may also look dull. It will have a flabby stomach area compared to the taught defined muscles of a fit animal. It could start to sweat. It can win but not very often.

The Sharp Horse

The horse's coat is shining, its well-defined muscles rippling as it walks. Its head may be tucked down, neck arched, ears pricked forward. It could appear agitated but not in an angry way. It's simply bright and keen to get on with the job and will often strut around the parade ring with exuberance. The horse could sweat a little with excitement but not profusely. If this horse is your selection back it with confidence.

The Winning Horse

This is the type of animal that wins most races. It exudes well-being and displays all the physical attributes of the sharp horse but is distinguished by its quieter more 'professional' attitude. It rarely sweats and responds well to handlers and jockey. It will move smoothly to post, head down and ears pricked, with long sweeping strides. The horse wants to run and knows its job. If not outclassed it should win or go close.

The Romantic Horse
No need to go into too much detail here but if you see a three year old colt showing all the signs of incipient colt-like behaviour - beware. If he should encounter a like-minded filly in the paddock and you see them extending their noses toward each other, you can write them both off. Their minds are not on the race!

The Big Horse
There is no question that tall horses are generally faster than smaller horses. They have longer strides. Big horses usually come off best in traffic problems and are better equipped to carry more weight. Big two year olds are generally more mature than their rivals. If your choice looks bigger than average, as well as looking fit, it's a good bet.

CHAPTER FIVE

A System for All Time?

Is there really a betting system that works consistently well, year after year, indefinitely? Unfortunately, I would have to say probably not. I have personally followed racing systems for years and experienced the frustration of checking out a set of criteria for several months, becoming more and more excited as 'paper profits' mount up. I would decide to check it out in hindsight and spend many hours with last year's newspapers and it still looked good! By this time the end of the current season was looming but I determine to follow it with real bets next year. The new season arrives and, sure enough, the strike rate and profits continue to impress so, from a modest bank, I follow the method to good effect. I now know for a fact that the system has performed well for at least three years and, eagerly anticipating the next season, decide to increase stakes and go for it. Once again steady profits roll in and I begin making plans to buy that villa in Barbados! Next season the results start to disappoint a little. I do OK but profits are well down on previous years. Never mind, it was probably just a 'glitch' - a mediocre spell sent to try me. The following year results are still very mixed however, and I do little better than break even. I've done OK and turned a decent profit but it's probably time to move on.

I believe most successful systems only have a 'shelf life' of a few years, although I have known some methods to make a dramatic comeback years later. The reasons for this are twofold.

Firstly, any good betting method will start to lose its potency if it is over used.

As more and more punters latch onto a particular idea or set of criteria, bookmakers will inevitably start to factor this into prices offered and returns will gradually diminish.

Secondly, and just as importantly, circumstances can change, especially in horseracing.
Let's look at just some of the changes that can happen within racing and the betting industry that can cause our system to eventually become redundant.

The very nature of racing can change over the years making the betting climate very different than say, ten years ago or more. The introduction and increasing popularity of All-Weather racing, for example, means that Flat racing now operates all year round - but conditions and styles of racing are very different during the winter months than on the turf. Similarly, summer National Hunt meetings, unknown until a few years ago, makes jump racing an all year round sport with no noticeable start or end to the season. A well-known criteria of many systems *'The horse must have had a run during the current season'* ceases to have as much meaning. Another very noticeable change in recent years is the increasing number of *valuable claiming races*. At one time these would tend to be rather 'lowly' affairs but nowadays they can equal good class handicaps in quality and change our perception of them as a betting medium.

In the heyday of big punters like *Alex Bird*, each-way betting in non-handicap races was advocated as the professional way to bet. Today, most pro's turn to straight win bets in handicap races for value. Bookmakers have long since ensured that there is very little point in backing the second favourite at depressed odds and only one fifth the odds for a place.

A lot of good methods use speed or handicap ratings experts. But past results can be overturned if your particular expert retires and a new man with new ideas takes over.

Training methods can change over a period of time. One good example - until the introduction of All-Weather racing in this country probably the majority of trainers adopted a 'rest' policy for their horses. Following a good run the horse might not be seen again on the racetrack for at least a couple of weeks. Nowadays, more and more trainers are running their charges again quickly - cashing in while the horse is fit and in form.

Many good systems follow certain stables at certain courses, but caution is always required if the trainer suddenly loses form. It is not unusual for even a top trainer to have a thoroughly bad year, for whatever reason, and past results suddenly mean very little.

At certain courses the track bias can be changed and a previously strong draw bias can be negated. A couple of recent examples - a high draw in sprint races at Thirsk was absolutely essential until they changed the watering system recently. The draw is still important but nothing like as vital as before. The new polytrack surface at Lingfield All-Weather course proved to be a lot fairer and made any draw bias less pronounced. So any system based on draw bias needs to be looked at and possibly updated on a regular basis.

The weather, a subject close to every British person's heart, can make a difference. If, as global warming experts tell us, our climate is becoming milder but *wetter*, firm ground horses are in danger of becoming disadvantaged.

This might sound alarmist but regular flood conditions over recent years have caused insurance companies to re-think their premiums. Perhaps with soft or heavy going conditions prevailing more often than before we should think seriously about building provisos regarding the going into our systems.

Strictly speaking this really should not be necessary. If a trainer knows his horse will not like today's underfoot conditions (and almost certainly lose) I believe his obligation to punters is to withdraw it from the race. All too often though, a sudden downpour will not deter the trainer from running his firm ground specialist just to give it a race or perhaps because the owners are at the track. If your wager has been struck in the morning when conditions were very different, you're left holding a very bad bet!

So, being aware of changing circumstances and the fact that systems can become over used, causing depressed prices, means we should always be prepared to move on or at least make changes and amendments to our selection methods.

Having said all this, the systems contained in this book should give you many years of sterling service, for two reasons.

1. They have all recently been written or updated so, in their current form, have not been over used.

2. They all contain sound logical criteria that will never date, needing only a small amendment occasionally.

In the next chapter we examine how the idea of 'system betting' has evolved over the last few decades.

CHAPTER SIX

The Pioneers

Tom Ainslie

Over thirty years ago in 1968, a revolution was started in America that has changed our perception of horserace betting ever since. The publication of *Ainslie's Complete Guide to Thoroughbred Racing* demonstrated that you could apply intellectual skill and logic, in the same way as you might approach bridge or chess, and that successful players could reap much greater rewards than any other game. Ainslie was the first real expert to show that racing form could be analysed in such a way so as to produce a winning formula for anyone who cared to take the time and trouble. It is amazing to think that, before him, there was no proper definitive guide for punters wishing to take part in one of the world's largest industries! The book inspired many Americans to adopt a different approach to their betting and some of these became professionals. A few even wrote their own books to further contribute to the sport. Inevitably, many of the original ideas contained in the *guide* were superseded, but these later authors would admit that it was Tom Ainslie who first showed the way.

Until quite recently, we in Britain were slow to take up this more scientific approach. The typical punter's bookshelf might have housed the odd biography about Lester Piggott or the Desert Orchid story. However, there were very few publications available to help him in his quest for winners. The lesson was clear - to attract new people into the game, they must be able to learn how to play with a reasonable degree of competence.

As stated, many of Tom's ideas may have become outdated over the last thirty years and, of course, they were all originally designed for American racing. The book is still an entertaining and informative read though, and many of his simple systems could still be applied to racing on this side of the pond. Here are some of his favourite ploys, condensed into a few sentences that could give you food for thought.

The Basic Components

Before operating any systematic method perform the following elimination process:

1. Eliminate horses that seem unsuited to the distance of today's race.
2. Eliminate horses that do not seem in sufficiently *sharp condition*. For example a horse coming back after a long lay-off.
3. Eliminate horses that seem *outclassed* in today's race.
4. Eliminate horses that seem at a serious disadvantage on today's going or in light of any *draw bias*.

Tom Ainslie then devoted a whole chapter, towards the end of his book, listing a total of sixty principles for successful system building. I have picked out a handful that seemed suitable for adapting to racing in the UK and could still be relevant today.

- **Look for horses that last ran within ten days but finished unplaced. Back the one that has previously won over today's distance in a race of the same class**. The recent losing race and the correct placement today suggest a betting coup, particularly if a top jockey is booked.
- **Back any horse that won its last race easily no more than seven days ago**. An easy winner is in peak form and the trainer seeks a repeat victory to cash in on the horse's fitness. Ensure that the horse is the only one of its kind in today's race and is not stepping up in class.
- **Back the contender that won or placed most recently**. The 'last out in the money' system was, possibly, the most popular of them all. What better clue to top form than a recent good performance?
- **Back the horse that was favourite in its last race but lost, providing it gained ground at the finish.** Perhaps the horse was victimized by lack of room or a badly judged ride. This type of beaten favourite can be a good bet providing it is running again quickly.
- **If the favourite did not win its last race, or goes to post higher than even money, back the second favourite provided that it is male and won its last race within the last five days**. Opposing the favourite in this way can find good priced winners.

- **Back a contender that raced twice in the past fourteen days but did not win, provided that it has won at today's distance and class at some time in the past three months**. A properly place animal fit enough to race three times in two weeks is fit enough to win, perhaps at a price.
- **Back the horse that is chosen by the majority of newspaper tipsters when no other horse in the race has raced more recently or has earned a higher speed rating in its last three races**. Fitness, speed and the high regard of experts should produce a high strike rate.

So, all these rules demonstrate sound enough thinking and variations of these criteria still find their way into methods used today.

The Flying Dutchman
During the late 1970's and early 80's *Che Van der Wheil* became a 'living legend' to many avid systemites via his numerous letters and articles published in the Sporting Chronicle Handicap Book's *Sports Forum.*
In the Second World War, Van der Wheil was a member of the Free Dutch Forces and 1945 found him in England, wounded and penniless, his immediate family lost. During his recuperation he received half-a-crown a week. His first two shillings and sixpence went onto a horse that won and, gradually over many years, he made racing pay. This was no 'flash in the pan' however, as the young 'VDW' had moved in affluent circles in the 1930's and had spent a lot of time in England successfully following the British racing scene.

Quite possibly, VDW never 'told all' in the pages of the Sports Forum, but he left enough clues to allow many punters to formulate a method that became known as 'The Key'. There are several versions of his methods and you may be familiar with some of them. Essentially, his approach to finding winners revolved around the following principles:

- Concentrate on the better class races where the more reliable and consistent horses can be found.
- 85% of all winners come from the first five in the betting forecast. Ignore the rest.
- Look for good <u>recent</u> form.
- Consistency is a vital ingredient so look for horses that know how to win and are usually found among the first 3 or 4 home whenever they contest a race.
- Proven ability is essential. What kind of race has the horse been winning in the past? Speed ratings can give further clues.
- <u>Class</u> - that all-important factor. No matter how genuine, is the horse outclassed today?

Van der Wheil constantly repeated his formula for successful betting:
CONSISTENT FORM + ABILITY (Class) + CAPABILITY + PROBABILITY + HARD WORK (from the punter) = WINNERS!

Some years ago I remember attempting to put VDW's principles into a workable 'method'. Here's what I came up with:

1. Only consider better class races - Group, Listed, Graded events or Class A, B or C.

2. Only consider the market leaders according to the betting forecast - first four in the betting for non-handicaps, first five for handicaps.

3. Eliminate any horse whose last run was more than thirty days ago.

4. Give a consistency rating to each horse by adding together its last three places in the form figures. The lower the total - the better the rating. (0 counts as 10).

5. Give an ability rating to each horse by dividing the total win prize money by the number of races won. Then divide this figure by 100 to achieve the rating. The higher the total - the better the rating.

6. Look at the prize money for the last race the horse contested and divide by 100. If today's prize money rating is lower, the horse is *dropping in class*.

7. Bet if one contender has a clear advantage on the ratings.

The Systems Man
During the eighties *Nick Mordin* was a freelance advertising writer with a strong interest in horse racing. He first came to the betting public's attention via a series of articles in the Sporting Life's *Weekender*

publication where he became known as the 'systems man'. In 1992 he published his best-known work 'Betting for a Living' and followed this up more recently with a new book 'Winning Without Thinking'. Both books rank among the better British racing publications and contain lots of good ideas for the systemite to work with. Nick denies being a 'systems expert' and does not agree with following methods blindly but, nevertheless, acknowledges that they can be a "brilliant educational shortcut to help you become more skilled at picking winners. Certainly bet on the horses they pick but always monitor results carefully to ensure the system is still working".

Throughout his work he continually stresses these important points:

- A profitable method must not follow the crowd. The goal of a system is not to pick winners but to identify a type of horse that the betting public underrates.
- The majority of successful systems only have a 'shelf life' of a few years until they become over used and redundant.
- If you can't describe a system in a short sentence the idea behind it may not be strong enough for long-term profits.
- Don't expect a system to continue working when the circumstances that gave rise to it change.
- Don't bend the rules of the system to fit the results.
- Always remember that the betting market will eventually adjust to take account of any successful method for identifying winners.
- *Avoid systems whose success is based on an inadequate sample of results.*

I concur with all of the above.

CHAPTER SEVEN

The Sharp End

Trainers

"If you want to do everything yourself you won't aspire to much. You have to surround yourself with the right people". Michael Tabor. 1999.

As far as we are concerned, trainers are the most important people in racing. (Apologies to owners and jockeys!).

Choosing a stable to follow, or more than one, is always a worthwhile exercise. It helps you specialise and think strategically as you get to know how your yard operates. Look for a good consistent strike rate of at least 15% over the past four or five years. Certain trainers do well at certain tracks so consult the Trainers Tables for individual meetings in the Racing Post. Alternatively Trainers4Courses by Ken Turrell is an excellent seasonal publication (see back of book). *Always ensure the trainer is currently in form.* This is easily assessed by consulting the Postdata column for each meeting. 1, 2 or 3 ticks are a plus. Beware of **x** - denoting poor recent form. It is a well known fact that a trainer who hits top form can be unstoppable for a period, with just about every horse from the stable running well - even the big priced un-fancied ones. Always take note of trainers' comments in race reports or interviews. You can pick up invaluable clues about future plans.

The larger well-established yards are where most of the top class reliable and consistent horses can be found. However, don't ignore the smaller operations but be aware that many of these can be 'gambling stables' and sometimes unpredictable. Often the only clue you will get is a significant market move just before the 'off'.

Top trainers, such as Mark Johnston, Sir Michael Stoute, John Gosden and Saeed Bin Suroor can be expected to win around 20% of the races they contest. But pay attention to any stable scoring this sort of strike rate. Season's statistics are published regularly in the Racing Post.

Jockeys
"You must remember we have these athletes called jockeys, who are known throughout the world, and people want to see these highly skilled men just as much as good horses".
Mike Watt (former agent to Lester Piggott) 1981.

It is certainly true that a top rider can make all the difference in a tight driving finish and, on occasions, it can truthfully be said that the jockey won the race - coaxing his mount home when a lesser pilot might have failed. However, any jockey is only as good as the rides he gets so I do not attach as much importance to the jockey as I do to trainers. Having said that, my confidence is always boosted if one of my selections is ridden by one of the top boys. On the minus side, top jockeys can be over-bet so their mounts can sometimes be poor value.

As with trainers, it is always worth consulting the Top Jockeys' table for each meeting in the Racing Post. Certain riders, not always the superstars, do well at certain smaller tracks. Experience on All-Weather courses, for example, can often prove an asset.

Always be on the lookout for 'the new kid on the block'. The rising star apprentice who can claim up to 7lb off the allotted weight in a handicap is often worth his claim in gold. Another tip. Watch out for top jockeys riding in a handicap at their *natural weight*.

You will find this information under *Seasons Statistics* in the Racing Post. It is always an advantage when the horse is not carrying dead weight in the form of lead in the saddlebags.

Top jockeys such as L. Dettori, K. Fallon and A.P. McCoy can be expected to win at least 20% of their races and make the frame around 50% of the time.

Tracks for Trainers
Certain trainers do consistently well at their favourite courses, making a level stake profit on all their runners. Research over four years revealed that you could have backed these trainers blindly and made huge profits at the following tracks. So, if our system selection has the right trainer at the right course this can only add to our confidence.

National Hunt Racing

- **Aintree** - J.J. O'Neill.
- **Ascot** - N.T. Chance, M.C. Pipe.
- **Ayr** - P.J. Hobbs, T.P. Tate, Mrs. L.C. Taylor, I.P. Williams.
- **Bangor** - Mrs. H. Dalton, A. King, Mrs. H.C. Knight, P.F. Nicholls, J.J. O'Neill, S.E.H. Sherwood, P.R. Webber, L. Wells.
- **Carlisle** - T.R. George, P.C. Haslam, J. Howard Johnson, I. Williams.
- **Cartmel** - D. Burchall, E.W. Tuer.
- **Cheltenham** - H. Daly.
- **Chepstow** - P.J. Hobbs, Miss Venetia Williams.
- **Doncaster** - T.D. Easterby, T.R. George, J.J. O'Neill, M.C. Pipe, T.P. Tate.
- **Exeter** - M. Bradstock, Mrs. S.D. Williams.
- **Fakenham** - N.T. Chance, N.J. Henderson, Mrs. S.P. Sly, Mrs. L. Wadham.
- **Folkestone** - Miss E.C. Lavelle, F. Murphy, S.E.H. Sherwood, Miss Venetia Williams.
- **Fontwell** - P.W. Hiatt, C.J. Mann, G.L. Moore, P.F. Nicholls, R. Rowe, Mrs. L.C. Taylor.
- **Haydock** - A. King, M. Todhunter.
- **Hereford** - N.J. Henderson, Miss H.C. Knight, Miss S.J. Wilton.
- **Hexham** - N.G. Richards, Miss L.C. Siddall, N. Twiston-Davies.
- **Huntingdon** - T.R. George, J.M. Jefferson, I. Williams, Miss Venetia Williams.
- **Kelso** - L. Lungo.

- **Kempton** - N.J. Henderson, P.R. Webber.
- **Leicester** - Miss E.C. Lavelle, C.J. Mann.
- **Market Rasen** - Mrs. L. Wadham
- **Musselburgh** - L. Lungo.
- **Newbury** - N.J. Henderson.
- **Newcastle** - R. Ford, P. Monteith.
- **Newton Abbot** - J.W. Mullins, P.F. Nicholls.
- **Perth** - G.M. Moore, Mrs. S.J. Smith, N. Twiston-Davies.
- **Plumpton** - R.H. Alner, N.T. Chance, N.J. Hawke, N.J. Henderson, Miss E.C. Lavelle, Mrs. N Smith.
- **Sandown** - P.R. Chamings, N.J. Henderson, P.F. Nicholls.
- **Sedgefield** - L. Lungo, M.C. Pipe.
- **Southwell** - P.J. Hobbs, N. Twiston-Davies, Miss Venetia Williams.
- **Stratford** - P.J. Hobbs, A. King.
- **Taunton** - R.T. Phillips, Miss Venetia Williams.
- **Uttoxeter** - N.A. Gaselee, F. Murphy, N.G. Richards, A. Turnell.
- **Warwick** - C.J. Mann
- **Wincanton** - P.F. Nicholls.
- **Worcester** - G.M. McCourt, P.F. Nicholls, S.E.H. Sherwood, Mrs. L. Wadham, Miss Venetia Williams.

Turf Flat Racing

- **Ascot** - Mark Johnston, M.P. Tregoning.
- **Ayr** - L.M. Cumani, Miss L.A. Perratt
- **Bath** - J. Akehurst.
- **Beverley** - W. Jarvis, Paul Johnson, Sir Mark Prescott, M. Quinlan, M.P. Tregoning.
- **Brighton** - G.A. Butler, R. Charlton, J.M.P. Eustace, P.J. Makin, B.R. Millman, C.F. Wall.
- **Carlisle** - W.H. Tinning.
- **Catterick** - J.M.P. Eustace, A. Turnell.
- **Chepstow** - H.C. Candy, E.A.L. Dunlop, P.W. Hiatt, B.J. Meehan, B. Palling.
- **Chester** - G.A. Butler, J.H.M. Gosden, P.J. Makin, J. Noseda, M.P.Tregoning.
- **Doncaster** - J.D. Bethell, M.J. Ryan, W.G.M. Turner.
- **Epsom** - H. Morrison, S.C. Williams.
- **Folkestone** - Alan Berry, D. Nicholls, J.W. Payne, M.G. Quinlan.
- **Goodwood** - S. Bin Suroor, J.G. Given, D.R. Loder, M.P. Tregoning.
- **Hamilton** - E.J. Alston, T.D. Barron, P.C. Haslam.
- **Haydock** - W.J. Haggas, M.A. Jarvis, J.A. Osborne.
- **Kempton** - H. Collingridge, M.C. Pipe.
- **Leicester** - P.W. D'Arcy, J.M.P. Eustace, J.R. Fanshawe.
- **Lingfield** - C.F. Wall.

- **Musselburgh** - M.L.W. Bell, G.A. Butler, R.M. Whitaker.
- **Newbury** - M.A. Jarvis, D.R. Loder, M.P. Tregoning.
- **Newcastle** - M. Channon, W.J. Haggas.
- **Pontefract** - J.R. Jenkins, Sir Michael Stoute.
- **Redcar** - L.M. Cumani, J. Noseda.
- **Ripon** - H.R.A. Cecil, P.F.I. Cole.
- **Salisbury** - J.H.M. Gosden, W.J. Haggas
- **Sandown** - N.A. Callaghan, H.C. Candy, P.F.I. Cole, J.J. Quinn, I. Semple, A.C. Stewart, S.C. Williams.
- **Thirsk** - J.A.R. Toller.
- **Warwick** - J. O'Reilly, Sir Michael Stoute.
- **Windsor** - Mark Johnston.
- **Yarmouth** - D.R. Loder.
- **York** – S. Bin Suroor.

Please note I am not suggesting that these are the only stables to follow at the individual courses but all the above were the most consistently profitable.

Amazingly, blindly following all the above trainers over four years made a massive level stake profit of 4,560 points or 1,140 a year! I would not necessarily recommend using this as a system in its own right but these figures are definitely food for thought and, as stated earlier, a real help in the final selection process.

For example, if our system selection is running at Chester and is trained by Gerard Butler our interest is immediately awakened. If we find that the horse has previously won over the same course and distance, has the going in its favour and is well drawn today we must be confident that we have found a strong selection worthy of a good bet.

CHAPTER EIGHT

Gold Dust in the Sand

All-Weather racing has come a long way since its introduction in 1989. It is now a significant part of the fixture list and, like it or not, the sand is here to stay. Traditionalists may be outraged but I foresee a day when we may boast a dozen or more tracks with artificial surfaces. Many of these could operate several days a week because, unlike turf, no recovery time is required. In recent years many serious punters have seen the betting opportunities available, whilst bookmakers freely admit to lower profits from the All-Weather. Many aspects of it can be more predictable than turf racing as the high percentage of winning favourites shows. In a recent interview high profile bookmaker Barry Dennis admitted that "the real players head to Lingfield, not Royal Ascot!" Pro punter Dave Nevison now makes All-Weather racing the mainstay of his betting. There is talk of higher prize money encouraging better quality racing. Lingfield has shown the way with their new *Polytrack* surface and results so far indicate that it can only help consistent form.

Many trainers and jockeys have become All-Weather specialists and it pays to follow these regular high percentage winners. Among the more successful trainers are: N.P. Littmoden, R. Hollinshead, P.D. Evans, K. Burke, Mrs. N. Macauley, T.D. Barron, P.C. Haslam, and G.L. Moore.

Some big stables, better known for their success on the turf, have successfully embraced the sand including: M. Johnston, B.W. Hills, J. Noseda, R. Hannon, G. Butler and Sir Mark Prescott. J.A. Osborne has already established a big reputation and strike rate with his All-Weather runners.

A study of the established All-Weather tracks revealed that certain trainers do consistently well, often at just one favoured course. Recent results, collected over three and a half years, show the most profitable trainers at each track, together with a breakdown of profit or loss in different types of races. The most profitable are highlighted in **bold**.

LINGFIELD (AW)

G.A. Butler
Total of 49 wins from 197 runs = 24.88%. Level Stake Profit = 34.22 points.
Handicaps 19 from 91 = 20.88%. Profit = +11.25
Claiming & Auction. 3 from 5 = 60%. Profit = = +12.
Maiden races. 15 from 67 = 22.39%. Loss = -13.20.
Other non-handicaps. 12 from 34 = 35.29%. Profit = +24.17.

J.H.M. Gosden
8 wins from 44 runs = 18.18%. LSP = 12.25.
Handicaps. 0 from 7 = 0%. Loss = -7.
Claiming & Auction. No runners.
Maiden races. 8 from 37 = 21.62%. Profit = +19.25.
Other non-handicaps. No runners.

B. Hanbury
6 wins from 23 runs =21.74%. LSP = 30.50.
Handicaps. 3 from 16 = 18.75%. Profit = +27.
Claiming & Auction. No runners.
Maiden races. 1 from 3 = 33.33%. Profit +1.50.
Other non-handicaps. 1 from 4 = 25%. Profit = +2.

P.W. Harris
13 wins from 80 runs = 16.25%. LSP = 57.83.
Handicaps. 9 from 45 = 20%. Profit = +71.
Claiming & Auction. No runners.
Maiden races. 3 from 26 = 11.54% Loss = -8.71.
Other non-handicaps. 1 from 9 = 11.11% Loss = -5.

P.C. Haslam
9 wins from 42 runs = 21.43%. LSP = 22.67.
Handicaps. 6 from 33 = 18%. Profit = +6.17.
Claiming & Auction. 3 from 6 = 50%. Profit = +19.50.
Maiden races. 0 form 1 = 0%. Loss = -1.
Other non-handicaps. 0 from 2 = 0%. Loss = -2.

A.P. Jarvis
15 wins from 121 runs = 12.40%. LSP = 52.
Handicaps. 8 from 74 = 10.81%. Profit = +20.
Claiming & Auction. 0 from 10 = 0%. Loss = -10.
Maiden races. 5 from 19 = 26.32%. Profit = +40.
Other non-handicaps. 2 from 18 = 11.11% Profit = +2.

M.A. Jarvis
8 wins from 45 runs = 17.78%. LSP = 16.41.

Handicaps. 2 from 19 = 10.53%. Loss = -6.50.
Claiming & Auction. 1 from 2 = 50%. Profit = +1.
Maiden races. 4 from 17 = 23.53%. Profit = +27.
Other non-handicaps. 1 from 7 = 14.29%. Loss = -5.09.

D.R. Loder
6 wins from 18 runs = 33.33%. LSP = 14.15.
Handicaps. 1 from 5 = 20%. Profit = +8.
Claiming & Auction. No runners.
Maiden races. 3 from 9 = 33.33%. Loss = -4.35.
Other non-handicaps. 2 from 4 = 50%. Profit +10.50.

G.L. Moore
55 wins from 388 runs = 14.18%. LSP = 0.37%.
Handicaps. 30 from 241 = 12.45%. Loss = -5.37.
Claiming & Auction. 13 from 36 = 36.11%. Profit = +32.37.
Maiden races. 4 from 51 = 7.84%. Loss = -34.55.
Other non-handicaps. 8 from 60 = 13.33%. Profit = +7.92.

SOUTHWELL (AW)

J. Balding
21 wins from 167 runs = 12.57%. LSP = 65.50.
Handicaps. 13 from 86 = 15.12%. Profit = +37.50.
Claiming & Auction. 4 from 30 = 13.33%. Profit = +46.
Maiden races. 0 from 20 = 0%. Loss = -20.
Other non-handicaps. 4 from 31 = 12.90%. Profit = +2.

T.D. Barron

71 wins from 327 runs = 21.71%. LSP = 76.28.
Handicaps. 33 from 184 = 17.93%. Profit = +39.37.
Claiming & Auction. 15 from 55 = 27.27%. Profit = +13.18.
Maiden races. 9 from 36 = 25%. Profit = +1.13.
Other non-handicaps. 14 from 52 = 26.92%. Profit = +22.60.

M.L.W. Bell

7 wins from 25 runs = 28%. LSP = 4.25.
Handicaps. 0 from 9 = 0%. Loss = -9.
Claiming & Auction. 0 from 1 = 0%. Loss = -1.
Maiden races. 5 from 11 = 45.45%. Profit = +11.
10 Other non-handicaps. 2 from 4 = 50%. Profit = +3.25.

W. Jarvis

14 wins from 54 runs = 25.93%. LSP = 43.53.
Handicaps. 7 from 27 = 25.93%. Profit = +37.98.
Claiming & Auction. 4 from 7 = 57.14%. Profit = +12.75.
Maiden races. 2 from 17 = 11.76. Loss = -8.70.
Other non-handicaps. 1 from 3 = 33.33%. Profit = +1.50.

H. Morrison

15 wins from 36 runs = 41.67%. LSP = 71.18.
Handicaps. 10 from 23 = 43.48%. Profit = +47.30.
Claiming & Auction. 3 from 6 = 50%. Profit = +20.13.
Maiden races. 1 from 4 = 25%. Profit = +4.

Other non-handicaps. 1 from 3 = 33.33%. Loss = -0.25.

B. Smart
23 wins from 159 runs = 14.47%. LSP 32.83.
Handicaps. 12 from 94 = 12.77%. Profit = +5.83.
Claiming & Auction. 1 from 10 = 10%. Profit = +11.
Maiden races. 8 from 38 = 21.05%. Profit = +21.50.
Other non-handicaps. 2 from 17 = 11.76. Loss = -5.50.

I.A. Wood
15 wins from 136 runs = 11.03%. LSP = 70.75.
Handicaps. 10 from 89 = 11.24%. Profit = +47.25.
Claiming & Auction. 2 from 20 = 10%. Profit = +9.
Maiden races. 0 from 4 = 0%. Loss = -4.
Other non-handicaps. 3 from 23 = 13.04%. Profit = +18.50.

WOLVERHAMPTON (AW)

P.W. D'arcy
10 wins from 43 runs = 23.26%. LSP = 23.75.
Handicaps. 6 from 28 = 21.43%. Profit = +17.75.
Claiming & Auction. 1 form 2 = 50%. Profit = +5.
Maiden races. 2 from 7 = 28.57%. Profit = +3.75.
Other non-handicaps. 1 from 6 = 16.67%. Loss = -2.75.

R. Guest
9 wins from 43 runs = 20.93%. LSP = 18.23.
Handicaps. 6 from 23 = 26.09%. Profit 20.23.
Claiming & Auction. 0 from 8 = 0%. Loss = -8.
Maiden races. 1 from 7 = 14.29%. Profit = +1.

Other non-handicaps. 2 from 5 = 40%. Profit = +5.

W.J. Haggas
15 wins from 62 runs = 24.19%. LSP = 5.46.
Handicaps. 7 from 31 = 22.58%. Profit = +11.01.
Claiming & Auction. 0 from 3 = 0%. Loss = -3.
Maiden races. 7 from 23 = 30.43%. Profit = +0.92.
Other non-handicaps. 1 from 5 = 20%. Loss = -3.47.

R. Hannon
17 wins from 94 runs = 18.09%. LSP = 6.35.
Handicaps. 11 from 58 = 18.97%. Profit = +13.55.
Claiming & Auction. 1 from 9 = 11.11%. Profit = +3.
Maiden races. 3 from 23 = 13.04%. Loss = -11.25.
Other non-handicaps. 2 from 4 = 50%. Profit = +1.05.

M.A. Jarvis
14 wins from 41 runs = 34.15%. LSP = 23.43.
Handicaps. 8 from 22 = 36.36%. Profit = +23.76.
Claiming & Auction. No runners.
Maiden races. 6 from 16 = 37.50%. Profit = +2.67
Other non-handicaps. 0 from 3 = 0%. Loss = -3.

W. Jarvis
11 wins from 41 runs = 26.83%. LSP = 22.74.
Handicaps. 4 from 19 = 21%. Profit = +20.50.
Claiming & Auction. 0 from 2 = 0%. Loss = -2.
Maiden races. 7 from 18 = 38.89%. Profit = +6.24.
Other non-handicaps. 0 from 2 = 0%. Loss = -2.

Miss Gay Kelleway
20 wins from 129 runs = 15.50%. LSP = 58.50.

Handicaps. 14 from 93 = 15%. Profit = +13.75.
Claiming & Auction. 0 from 6 = 0%. Loss = -6.
Maiden races. 4 from 17 = 23.53%. Profit = +55.50.
Other non-handicaps. 2 from 13 = 15.38%. Loss = -4.75.

N.P. Littmoden
90 wins from 579 runs = 15.54%. LSP = 7.10.
Handicaps. 53 from 352 = 15%. Profit = +16.74.
Claiming & Auction. 17 from 63 = 26.98%. Profit = +29.37.
Maiden races. 2 from 13 = 15.38%. Loss = -8.42.
Other non-handicaps. 1 from 9 = 11/11%. Loss = -5.50.

P.J. Makin
16 wins from 69 runs = 23.19%. LSP = 34.96.
Handicaps. 9 from 40 = 22.50%. Profit = +38.88.
Claiming & Auction. 4 from 7 = 57.14%. Profit = +10.
Maiden races. 2 from 13 = 15.38%. Loss = -8.42.
Other non-handicaps. 1 from 9 = 11.11%. Loss = -5.50.

Statistics such as these can serve as an extremely useful reference when making our selections. For example, you would have extra confidence in a selection running at Wolverhampton in a handicap or claimer that was trained by N.P. Littmoden. But you would not want to support his horses running in maiden or other non-handicap races.

A big list of 'sand specialists' could be compiled from the jockeys but you would have to include J. Quinn, Martin Dwyer, D. Holland, E. Ahern, Dane O'Neill, P.

Doe, N. Callan, S. Whitworth, I. Mongan, C. Catlin, T.G. McLaughlin, & Dean McKeown. Many talented apprentices do particularly well on the All-Weather and are quickly establishing names for themselves. Joanna Badger, G. Gibbons & J.F. McDonald are just three among many worthy of mention who started their careers on the All-Weather tracks as apprentices but now rank among the top riders. **An apprentice's weight allowance can be particularly valuable on the All-Weather** because races are often run at a fast early pace and are not so much a test of tactical skill or strength in the saddle.

There seems little doubt that the pedigree of a horse is important when it comes to this different style of racing.

There are certain sires whose progeny are particularly suited to racing on artificial surfaces rather than turf. There are many speculations about the reasons for this but one important attribute has to be speed. If a horse hasn't got enough speed in its pedigree it is likely to get left behind in the early rush. Here is a list of stallions you should watch out for in the breeding of your All-Weather horse.

Alzao	Petorius
Ballad Rock	Perugino
Be My Guest	Polar Falcon
Bold Arrangement	Polish Patriot
Cadeaux Genereux	Priolo
Caerleon	Rainbow Quest
Damister	Red Sunset

Dayjur
Dowsing
Effisio
Ela-Mana-Mou
Green Desert
Kalaglow
Keen
Key of Luck
Last Tycoon
Lugana Beach
Most Welcome
Pennine Walk
Petong

Rock City
Roi Danzig
Royal Academy
Sayf el Arab
Sharrood
Sure Blade
Unfuwain
Warning
Warrshan
Wolfhound
Woodborough
Woodman

Alternatively, there are certain sires to <u>avoid</u> on the All-Weather. The following stallions, all with brilliant turf progeny, simply do not produce offspring to suit the sand.

High Estate
Polish Precedent
Sadler's Well

Inchinor
Slip Anchor

The last named has to be one of the most successful stallions of all time - but don't follow him on the All-Weather.

Finally, here are a few good betting guidelines quoted by leading All-Weather trainer T.D. Barron.

- Don't bet that a horse will win its first race on sand. It normally takes a run or two before the horse gets used to the new surface.

- Concentrate your bets on the trainers who have learned how to train winners on the surface - those who consistently appear at the head of the trainer's table for the track.

- A horse that has run well on firm ground on grass is more likely to adapt to an artificial surface than a turf runner that prefers soft going.

- At Southwell, on the five furlong course, give an edge to the horse with a low draw. They are racing on the most used (and firmest) part of the track.

- Pay more attention to jockeys than you normally would. Certain jockeys have really got the knack of riding the All-Weather tracks.

Conclusions are that All-Weather racing is still a rather specialized field so it pays to follow top trainers, top jockeys including apprentices, top sires and horses that can show early speed, particularly front runners - those that can hit the front early and stay there. All-Weather racing can be perfect for system betting because of the more consistent surface. At the time of writing there are several proposed new All-Weather tracks currently under construction or in the planning stage. There is little doubt then that All-Weather racing is very much on the up-grade and could soon be on a par with the best quality turf racing. With the introduction of the favoured Polytrack surface we can now look forward to quality racing on artificial surfaces all year round giving tremendous betting opportunities for anyone wishing to specialise.

CHAPTER NINE

The Arithmetic of Racing

There is a very old principle in horserace betting that keeps cropping up in various systems. Many years ago this method of betting was known as 'dutching' - supposedly in honour of its originator known as Dutch. His exploits were, apparently, legendary on American racetracks before the days of mutuel machines when a hustler could shop among the trackside bookmakers for the best odds. Knowledgeable punters made money by betting on every horse in the race except rank outsiders, over-rated favourites and other animals that figured to lose. Its basis was the bookmakers' scale of percentages. For an easy example, if the player felt that an even-money choice could not win he would operate as if half the betting pool was up for grabs because the 'false' favourite was taking up 50% of the market. Simply by betting on every other horse in the race, in amounts equal or proportionate to their price percentage, he could win a substantial amount.

Now this idea can make a lot of sense. The bookmaker makes his profit by covering every horse in the race and, in theory at least, he gains whichever horse wins. 'Dutching' plays the bookmaker at his own game in a way, although we do not bet on every horse. A lot of races can be successfully narrowed down to just two, three or four runners from which we can be pretty sure the winner will come - barring accidents. Betting on these runners, in varying amounts depending on the odds offered, can be a rewarding way of doing things. The key to success is finding the right race. Ideally, we need a good quality affair with, say, no more than twelve runners.

We decide that, all things being equal, we cannot imagine that the winner will not be found outside of the first three in the betting. We back all three and look for a return of approximately 100 points whichever wins. For example, if the favourite is quoted at 3/1, the second favourite at 4/1, the third favourite at 6/1 and the rest at 10/1 or over, then we have a good opportunity. By consulting the table on the next page you will see that we stake £25 on the favourite at 3/1, £20 on the second favourite at 4/1 and £15 on the third favourite at 6/1. So, our total stake is £60. If the favourite wins our return is £100 - a profit of £40. If the 4/1 shot wins our return is the same with a profit of £40. If the 6/1 shot wins our return is £105 - a profit of £45. We can't lose, providing we find the right race and are not surprised by an outsider!

In the odds percentage table you will see that stakes are based on the percentage figures but rounded up to avoid betting in pence. For ease of operation, I would be inclined to round up to the nearest fiver - a bet of £39 would be bound to cause a raised eyebrow from your friendly bookie! You can bet on as many horses in one race as you think necessary providing the total stake is no more than £80. This way you ensure a profit of at least 20%. Anything less than this is not worthwhile, so our example of three horses at 3/1, 4/1 &

6/1 is ideal but 6/4, 2/1 & 4/1 is not. When the odds are not right simply leave that race alone.

(By the way, the table can also be useful in working out how many winners you need from one hundred bets to secure a profit within a certain price range. For example, if your selections are at a price of 6/4 you will need forty winners to break even. If you normally bet within the price range of, say, 2/1 to 7/2 you will need approximately 27% winners to break even).

So, we should never be afraid of backing more than one horse in the same race, providing the odds are right.

Odds	% Profitability	Stake
Evens	50.00	£50
11/10	47.62	£48
6/5	45.45	£46
5/4	44.44	£45
11/8	42.11	£43
6/4	40.00	£40
13/8	38.10	£39
7/4	36.36	£37
15/8	34.78	£35
2/1	33.33	£34
85/40	32.00	£32
9/4	30.77	£31
5/2	28.57	£29
11/4	26.67	£27
3/1	25.00	£25
10/3	23.08	£24
7/2	22.22	£23

Odds	% Profitability	Stake
4/1	20.00	£20
9/2	18.18	£19
5/1	16.67	£17
11/2	15.38	£16
6/1	14.29	£15
13/2	13.33	£14
7/1	12.50	£13
15/2	11.76	£12
8/1	11.11	£12
17/2	10.53	£11
9/1	10.00	£10
10/1	9.09	£10
11/1	8.33	£9
12/1	7.69	£8
14/1	6.67	£7
16/1	5.88	£6
20/1	4.76	£5
25/1	3.85	£4
33/1	2.94	£3

CHAPTER TEN

Percentages & Statistics

There are many aspects of horseracing that are really quite predictable. The following percentages will vary only slightly from year to year.

- 20% of all horses in training win over 80% of all races.

We should focus on this small group of reliable and consistent types. If there were, say, 200 horses running on a particular day, only around 40 would be worthy of our consideration - narrowing the field down nicely to start with.

- 32% of all Flat races are won by the favourite.

Around 25% win handicaps and 40% win non-handicaps.

These percentages generally increase for National Hunt racing because jump horses can be more consistent than their Flat counterparts.

Consider the following tables, covering a five year period they show us that around 74% of all Flat races are won by one of the first four in the betting.

Non-Handicaps	Win%	Aggregate
1st Favourites	38.8	38.8
2nd Favs.	20.1	58.9
3rd Favs.	13.2	72.1
4th Favs.	8.5	80.6

Handicaps	Win%	Aggregate
1st Favs.	25.2	25.2
2nd Favs.	16.5	41.7
3rd Favs.	12.6	54.3
4th Favs.	9.4	63.7

Two Year Olds	Win%	Aggregate
1st Favs.	36.8	36.8
2nd Favs.	19.8	56.6
3rd Favs.	12.4	69
4th Favs.	8.2	77.2

However, percentages of winning favourites can vary considerably depending upon a number of other factors, as the following tables show.

First favourite Statistics

By No. Runners	Handicap Win%	Non-Handicap Win %
Less Than 5	50	57.1
5-7	33.7	45.1
8-12	27.5	37.2
12-15	22.7	30.6
16+	18.4	30.6

By Race Distance

Less than 6.5f	23.5	37.1
6.5 – 9.5f	24.3	38.2

9.5 – 12.5f	26.9	40.9
12.5 – 16.5f	27.6	46.8
16.5+	30.1	46.7

By Time of Year

Early season	20	33.4
May	23.7	37.6
June	27.8	38.8
July	29.7	41.9
August	25.9	40.9
September	23.3	38.3
Oct / Nov	22.2	38.4
All-Weather	25	39.3

By Going

Heavy	22.4	34.6
Soft	22.8	34.3
Good / Soft	24.6	34.2
Good	24.6	38.7
Good / Firm	25.3	40.9
Firm	27.9	41.2
Hard	25.6	39.7

By Previous Position

First	30.1	46.5
Second	25	40.4
Third	20.7	37.7
Fourth	23	36.1

By Course

Winning favourite percentages can also vary widely from track to track. This information is available every day in the form of a *Favourites Box* for each meeting in the Racing Post. You can see, at a glance, how favourites have performed, in different types of races, over the past four years. In fact, you can use this to help identify 'good favourites' by noting any type of race at the course where the strike rate is 40% or more. The following league table of winning percentages for all starting price favourites at each course was compiled over a five years period.

Winning Favourite Percentages (Course by Course)

Flat Racing

Thirsk	36.6%	Wolverhampton*	31.11%
Chester	36%	Musselburgh	30.78%
Ripon	34.22%	Nottingham	30.77%
Folkestone	34.19%	Doncaster	30.75%
Yarmouth	34.04%	Goodwood	30.17%
Southwell^	33.77%	Newcastle	29.95%
Hamilton	33.16%	Southwell*	29.76%
Lingfield^	32.42%	Newmarket (July)	29.64%
Brighton	32.23%	York	29.63%
Beverley	32.14%	Haydock	29.48%
Carlisle	32.13%	Sandown	29.34%
Bath	32.08%	Epsom	29.16%
Catterick	32%	Pontefract	29.08%
Ayr	31.69%	Windsor	28.87%
Leicester	31.66%	Newbury	28.8%

Warwick	31.54%	Redcar	28.70%
Salisbury	31.49%	Newmarket (Rowley)	28.02%
Lingfield*	31.23%	Chepstow	27.32%
Kempton	31.11%	Ascot	25.83%

*All-Weather   ^Turf

National Hunt Racing

Folkestone	38.87%	Ludlow	34.08%
Ayr	37.78%	Sedgefield	34%
Haydock	37.11%	Lingfield	33.93%
Wincanton	37.09%	Carlisle	33.74%
Wetherby	37.02%	Leicester	33.65%
Uttoxeter	36.08%	Huntingdon	33.50%
Hereford	36%	Warwick	33.42%
Newton Abbot	35.60%	Sandown	33.3%
Fakenham	35.52%	Newcastle	33.3%
Hexham	35.41%	Market Rasen	33.18%
Bangor	35.19%	Cheltenham	33%
Musselburgh	35.17%	Kempton	32.87%
Kelso	35.11%	Towcester	32.81%
Chepstow	34.88%	Stratford	32.80%
Southwell	34.84%	Catterick	32.66%
Plumpton	34.65%	Newbury	32.20%
Perth	34.51%	Fontwell	31.58%
Taunton	34.43%	Doncaster	31.05%
Exeter	34.25%	Ascot	30.41%
Worcester	34.19%	Aintree	24.88&
		Cartmel	24%

More Powerful Statistics

Weight - 66% of all winners carry no more weight than their last run.

Recent Form - 53% of all winners won or placed in their last race.

Distance - 60% of winners ran at the same distance as their last race.

The Market
- 30% of winners start at 2/1 or less.
- 45% of winners start at 3/1 or less.
- 65% of winners start at 5/1 or less.
- 78% of winners start at 7/1 or less.

(The price bracket 13/8 to 6/1 produces over 52% winners so you are not missing very much leaving alone very short prices. However, you need a good reason to back at 8/1 or over).

- 67% of winners come from the first three in the betting.
- One of the first three in the betting is placed 90% of the time.
- 87% of winners are returned at odds *less than the number of runners.*

Here are some more interesting statistics that show the average price of winners in different types of races.

Race Type	Average Price of Winners
3 year old maidens	11/4
Conditions events	9/2
2 year old maidens	5/1
Classified races	7/1
Group/Listed races	7/1
Claiming races	7/1
Selling races	7/1
Stakes races	15/2
Apprentice/Amateur races	17/2
Middle distance handicaps	17/2
Staying handicaps	9/1
Nurseries	10/1
Sprint handicaps	11/1

The higher the average price the harder it is to predict the outcome of that particular type of race. So the more predictable races are three year-old maidens and Conditions races whilst Nurseries (handicaps for two year-olds) and Sprint Handicaps can produce erratic results and are best avoided.

Five Day Trainers
In recent years many trainers are running their horses again quickly to capitalize on their good recent form and fitness.

A very interesting set of figures, based on ten years results, show that certain trainers are more successful at doing this than others. I looked at trainers running their horses again within five days after a previous good run. All the trainers listed made a profit from a strike rate of at least 20%. The following figures provides some interesting food for thought, as do all these statistics that can form the basis of many a good system's criteria.

Trainers Who Are Successful When Running Horses Again Within Five Days

Trainers	Runs	Wins	Win%	Profit
R.M. Whitaker	64	13	20.3	57.25
K.R. Burke	45	10	22.2	51.80
M.H. Tomkins	64	13	20.3	22.07
B.A. McMahon	21	5	23.8	21.50
K. McAuliffe	15	3	20	20.17
J. Pearce	37	8	21.6	19
S.E. Kettleworth	24	6	25	14.50
Sir Mark Prescott	47	15	31.9	10.23
M.L.W. Bell	24	7	29.2	9.80
Jamie Poulton	14	3	21.4	7.75
D.W.P. Arbuthnot	21	5	23.8	7.38
B.R. Millman	11	3	27.3	6
A.G. Newcombe	16	4	25	6
D. Haydn Jones	15	5	33.3	4.88
C.W. Thornton	21	6	28.6	2.75
I.A. Balding	18	4	22.2	2.50

Where To Follow Favourites

Flat Statistics
Percentages based on winning favourites tend to remain pretty constant from year to year. However

percentages can vary quite considerably from course to course. These statistics cover a five years period and *avoided* heavy going conditions and races with more than sixteen runners. I came up with two useful lists for all Flat racing. 'Favourites to Follow' shows you courses where unusually high percentages (over 45%) have won in certain types of races. Favourites to Avoid highlights low winning percentages of less than 20%. Being aware of these figures can help us to view the overall picture when assessing a particular race and help us to make decisions on whether to back or oppose the favourite.

Favourites to Follow

- **Ayr** - 2yo Maiden 45.3%. 3yo+ Listed 60%. 3yo Maiden 51.7%.
- **Bath** - 3yo+ Listed 50%. 3yo+ Stakes 46.8%. 3yo Maiden 49.1%.
- **Beverley** - 2yo Stakes 47%. 2yo Maiden 50%.
- **Brighton** - 2yo Stakes 50%. 2yo Maiden 47.5%. 3yo Maiden 52.7%.
- **Carlisle** - 3yo+ Claiming 61.1%.
- **Catterick** - 3yo+ Claiming 45.2%.
- **Chepstow** - 2yo Stakes 50%. 2yo Claiming 50%.3yo Maiden 58.1%.
- **Chester** - 2yo Stakes 59.3%. 2yo Maiden 60%. 3yo+ Group 57.1%. 3yo+ Claiming 50%. 3yo Maiden 54.5%.
- **Doncaster** - 2yo Maiden 49.3%. 3yo+ Stakes 48.7%.

- **Epsom** - 2yo Maiden 48.7%. 3yo+ Claiming 46.2%. 3yo Maiden 60%.
- **Folkestone** - 2yo Nursery 66.7%. 3yo Maiden 45%.
- **Goodwood** - 2yo Maiden 45.1%.
- **Hamilton** - 2yo Stakes 55.6%. 2yo Maiden 46.4%. 3yo Maiden 51.55.
- **Haydock** - 3yo+ Group 46.7%. 3yo+ Stakes 50%.
- **Kempton** - 2yo Stakes 47.6%. 3yo+ Group 100%.
- **Leicester** - 2yo Maiden 45%. 3yo Maiden 48%.
- **Lingfield (Turf)** - 2yo Claiming 46.2%. 3yo+ Listed 50%. 3yo+ Stakes 47.1%.
- **Lingfield (AW)** - 3yo+ Listed 66.7%. 3yo+ Claiming 45%.
- **Musselburgh** - 2yo Stakes 45%. 3yo Maiden 47.1%.
- **Newcastle** - 3yo+ Group 50%. 3yo Maiden 47.6%.
- **Nottingham** - 2yo Maiden 50%.
- **Pontefract** - 2yo Listed 50%. 2yo Stakes 66.7%.
- **Redcar** - 3yo Claiming 55%. 3yo Maiden 45.8%.
- **Ripon** - 2yo Stakes 57.7%. 2yo Maiden 46.5%. 3yo Maiden 65.2%.
- **Salsibury** - 2yo Claiming 50%. 3yo+ Stakes 50%.
- **Sandown** - 2yo Maiden 45%. 3yo+ Stakes 53.3%. 3yo+ Claiming 50%.
- **Thirsk** - 3yo Maiden 51.5%.
- **Warwick** - 2yo Stakes 66.7%. 2yo Maiden 50.8%. 3yo+ Stakes 45%. 3yo Maiden 50%.
- **Windsor** - 3yo+ Group 80%. 3yo Maiden 45%.
- **Yarmouth** - 2yo Maiden 48.5%. 3yo Maiden 49.2%.
- **York** - 2yo Listed 46.7%. 2yo Stakes 54.5%. 3yo+ Group 45%. 3yo+ Stakes 52.6%. 3yo Maiden 60%.

Favourites to Avoid

- **Ascot** - 3yo+ Listed 19.2%. Handicaps 17.9%.
- **Bath** - 2yo Nurseries 0%.
- **Beverley** - 2yo Nurseries 16.7%.
- **Brighton** - 2yo Claiming 14.3%.
- **Catterick** - 2yo Nurseries 19.2%.
- **Chepstow** - 3yo+ Handicaps 14.1%.
- **Doncaster** - All Claiming races 7.2%.
- **Epsom** - 2yo Nurseries 10%. 3yo+ Handicaps 17.1%.
- **Folkestone** - 2yo Stakes 9.1%.
- **Haydock** - 2yo Claiming 16.7%. 2yo Nurseries 14.3%.
- **Kempton** - 2yo Nurseries 14.3%.
- **Leicester** - 3yo+ Group or Listed 15%.
- **Musselburgh** - 2yo Nurseries 18.2%.
- **Newbury** - 2yo Nurseries 11.8%.
- **Newcastle** - 3yo+ Claiming 16.7%.
- **Redcar** - 2yo Claiming 0%. 2yo Nurseries 10.5%.
- **Ripon** - 2yo Nurseries 0%.
- **Salisbury** - 3yo+ Claiming 13.3%.
- **Sandown** - 2yo Group 0%. 3yo+ Handicaps 19.9%.
- **Thirsk** - 2yo Nurseries
- **Warwick** - 2yo Nurseries 12.5%. 3yo+ Claiming 13.3%.
- **Windsor** - 3yo+ Handicaps 18.6%.
- **York** - 3yo+ Claiming 10%. 3yo+ Handicaps 19.9%.

Obviously our list of 'Favourites to Follow' will not necessarily make you an overall profit backing them blindly but it can serve as a useful guide. Our list of 'Favourites to Avoid' could be very helpful if you like to lay horses on the Betting Exchanges.

National Hunt Statistics

In National Hunt races we know that the strike rate of market leaders tends to be higher than for Flat racing. As previously mentioned Flat horses generally hold their form for shorter periods because of the extra amount of energy required to win at a fast pace - especially over sprint distances. Jump horses are older, tougher individuals and are more capable of repeating good performances for longer. It is interesting to see how percentages can vary from course to course when we look at favourites and individual trainer's performances. The following list of National Hunt tracks are where *unusually high percentages* were recorded over a five years period.

- **Ayr** - Favourites win 50% of all Novice Hurdles & Novice Chases.
- **Catterick** - Favourites win 52% Novice Chases & 45% Novice Hurdles.
- **Doncaster** - Favourites win 56% Novice Hurdle races.
  Trainer K.C. Bailey wins 50% Handicap Chases contested.
- **Musselburgh** - Favourites win 54% Novice Hurdles & 44% Novice Chases.

Trainer F. Murphy wins 50% Novice Hurdles contested.

- **Exeter** - Favourites win 50% Novice Hurdles, 45% Novice Chases & 54% NH Flat races.
- **Fakenham** - Favourites win 57% Novice Chases & 47% Novice Hurdles.
  Trainers Mrs. P. Sly & O. Brennan each win 40% Handicap Chases they contest.
- **Folkestone** - Favourites win 60% Novice Chases & 50% Novice Hurdles.
- **Fontwell** - Favourites win 56% Novice Chases.
  In Novice Chases Miss V. Williams wins 50% and P.F. Nicholls 48%. M.C. Pipe wins 67% Selling Hurdles.
- **Haydock** - Favourites win 52% Novice Hurdles & 47% Novice Chases.
  Miss V. Williams wins 67% of all Novice Hurdles & Novice Chases and M.C. Pipe 50% Novice Chases.
- **Hereford** - Favourites win 60% Novice Hurdles & 51% Novice Chases.
  Better than average performances from K.C. Bailey - 50% Novice Chases, Miss H.C. Knight - 47% Handicap Hurdles, M.J.M. Evans - 50% Handicap Chases & N.J. Henderson - 50% Novice Hurdles.
- **Hexham** - Favourites win 54% Novice Hurdles.
- **Huntingdon** - Favourites win 52% of all non-handicap Hurdle races and all Novice Chases.
- **Kelso** - Favourites win 52% Novice Hurdles & 49% Novice Chases.
- **Kempton** - Favourites win 48% Novice Chases.
  N.J. Henderson has a 55% strike rate in Novice Chases.

- **Leicester** - Favourites win 52% of all non-handicap Hurdle races and 49% Novice Chases.
  C.J. Mann wins 50% Handicap Hurdles and M.C. Pipe 43% Novice Chases & 64% Selling Hurdles.
- **Lingfield** - Favourites win 66% Novice Hurdles & 57% Novice Chases.
- **Ludlow** - Favourites win 53% Novice Hurdles.
  M.C. Pipe wins 49% of all Novice Hurdles he contests.
- **Market Rasen** - Favourites win 50% Novice Chases & 48% Novice Hurdles.
  50% winners were achieved by J.R. Best in Handicap Hurdles and M.C. Pipe in Novice Chases.
- **Newbury** - Favourites win 56% Novice Chases.
- **Newcastle** - Favourites win 61% Novice Chases.
- **Newton Abbot** - Favourites win 56% of all non-handicap Hurdle races and 51% Novice Chases.
  M.C. Pipe has a 50% success rate in claiming hurdle races.
- **Plumpton** - Favourites win 53% Novice Chases & 49% Novice Chases.
  M.C. Pipe has a 52% strike rate in both these types of races.
- **Sandown** - Favourites win 57% Novice Hurdles.
  M.C. Pipe wins 59% of these races he contests.
- **Sedgefield** - Favourites win 53% NH Flat races & 47% Novice Chases.
- **Southwell** - Favourites win 63% Novice Hurdles.
- **Stratford** - Favourites win 52% Novice Hurdles.
  M.C. Pipe has a 48% strike rate in these races.

- **Taunton** - Favourites win 48% of all Novice and Selling Hurdle races.
- **Towcester** - Favourites win 59% of all Selling Hurdle races.
  R.H. Buckler won 70% of all Handicap Chases he contested.
- **Uttoxeter** - Favourites win 59% Novice Chases. Coincidentally the same 59% is recorded by P.F. Nicholls in these races.
- **Warwick** - Trainer P.F. Nicholls also scores highly here with 62% winners in Novice Chases. R. Dickin has a 50% strike rate in these races.
- **Wetherby** - Favourites win 51% Novice Chases and 54% NH Flat races.
  Trainer C. Grant scored 5 times out of 10 with his Handicap Chasers.
- **Wincanton** - Favourites win 58% Novice Chases.
- **Worcester** - Favourites do not have very high strike rates here but trainer C.J. Mann is worth a mention with a 55% strike rate in Novice Hurdle races.

Obviously these high percentages don't necessarily mean easy profits because prices are invariably depressed and often odds-on. Being aware of these figures, however, can help us to view the overall picture when assessing a particular race, even if it only means thinking carefully before opposing a favourite or certain trainer.

Of course, statistics like these require updating regularly but they can be the very essence of good racing systems. We are in the business of trying to predict the future and, in the absence of tomorrow's newspaper, all we have to go on is what happened in the past.

Providing our statistics are logically sound and based upon a lengthy period of results, we should expect certain percentages to repeat themselves with a reasonable degree of consistency.

The recommended systems that follow in Part Two of this book are all based upon this principle. They all contain sound logical criteria and can be relied upon to find a regular supply of winners all year round for Turf Flat, All-Weather and National Hunt racing. All have been thoroughly tested for at least three years and a full analysis of results is given showing annual strike rate, level stake profits and return on investment.

Part Two

THE RACING INVESTMENT PROGRAMME

~A Collection of Proven Systems~

RACING INVESTMENTS

~A Winning Strategy for Flat Racing~

There are certain types of non-handicap races on the Flat where the favourite will win often enough to show a consistent profit.

We only bet in the following types of non-handicap races:

- Claiming Races
- Selling Races
- Maiden Races
- Conditions Races for Two-Year Olds Only

We then follow four simple rules:

1. The race must have 5, 6 or 7 runners.
2. The horse must be no more than 7 years old.
3. The horse should be the clear favourite just before the off.
4. The price should be evens or better - do not bet odds-on.

This very simple strategy has made good profits over the last four years from an average strike rate of 43%. Losing runs will never be high so a sensible staking plan could enhance profits further. A full analysis of results over four years is included.

Racing Investments' System Logic

These types of non-handicap races are often bet on by on-course professionals who usually have a shrewd idea of the likely winner. Waiting until a clear favourite emerges ensures we are on the right horse. It is not advisable to take short odds-on prices because most of the time we will simply be turning money over with no real gain.

Concentrating on races with just five to seven runners ensures that our horse has fewer rivals and is unlikely to meet with traffic problems or be disadvantaged by any draw bias at the track.

Restricting bets to horses aged no more than seven ensures that our selection is unlikely to be on the downgrade.

Racing Investments System Results

2000 - 105 wins from 247 bets = 42.51% strike rate. Level Stake Profit = 31.07 points. Return on Investment = 12.58%.

2001 - 87 wins from 208 bets = 41.83% strike rate. Level Stake Profit = 24.19 points. Return on Investment = 11.63%.

2002 - 91 wins from 213 bets = 42.72% strike rate. Level Stake profit = 16.63 points. Return on Investment = 7.81%.

2003 - 106 wins from 235 bets = 45.11% strike rate. Level Stake Profit = 38.45 points. Return on Investment = 16.36%.

4 years total - 389 wins from 903 bets = 43.08% strike rate.
LSP = 110.34 points. ROI = 12.22%.
Longest winning run 7. Longest losing run 9.
Average winning starting price 13/8.

SUMMER SHADES

~Flat Racing System~

Horses wearing first-time headgear are often considered to be unreliable betting propositions. However, under certain circumstances, they can be very profitable to follow.

There are four simple rules:

1. Only consider Flat racing during the height of the season - during June, July and August.

2. The horse must be quoted as the Forecast Favourite in the Racing Post.

3. The horse must be blinkered or visored for the first time. (*Consult the information to the right of the race card in the Racing Post. Look for the abbreviation b1 or v1*).

4. The horse must have had at least one previous run during the current season. (*Consult the form figures next to the horse's name to the left of the race card. A small dash among these figures indicates previous season's form so the horse would not qualify if the form figures looked something like 253- indicating last season's form*).

Results over six seasons show an average strike rate of 42.68% and a good return on investment of 54.70%. Regular profits were achieved from starting prices up to

7/1. If you are not averse to backing odds-on it is worth noting that every horse returned at less than evens won - a strike rate of 100%!

Summer Shades' System Logic

The application of headgear is often taken as a sign that the horse may be 'quirky' or unreliable. However, trainers will often fit blinkers or visor to good horses with ability in an attempt to sharpen them up and concentrate their mind at the finish. When the horse is quoted as the favourite we presume that the odds compiler regards it as the best animal in the race and the headgear has been applied to go for a win.

Betting mid-season on the Flat is always the best time and ensuring that the horse has had a previous recent run means we can be reasonably confident regarding its fitness.

Summer Shades System Results

1998 - 11 wins from 23 bets = 47.83% strike rate.
Level Stake Profit = 14.68 points. Return on Investment = 63.83%

1999 - 11 wins from 23 bets = 47.83% strike rate.
Level Stake Profit = 18.90 points. Return on Investment = 82.17%.

2000 - 10 wins from 25 bets = 40% strike rate.
Level Stake Profit = 14.21 points. Return on Investment = 56.84%.

2001 - 8 wins from 28 bets = 28.57% strike rate.
Level Stake Profit = 6.75 points. Return on Investment = 24.11%.

2002 - 11 wins from 31 bets = 35.48% strike rate.
Level Stake Profit = 8.83 points. Return on Investment = 28.48%.

2003 - 19 wins from 34 bets = 55.88% strike rate.
Level Stake Profit = 26.34 points. Return on Investment = 77.47%.

6 years total - 70 wins from 164 bets = 42.68 strike rate.
LSP = 89.71 points. ROI = 54.70%
Longest winning run 5. Longest losing run 6.
Average winning starting price 5/2.

ALL-WEATHER GOOD THINGS

~Reliable Profits From Flat Racing On The Sand~

This method finds favourites that win around 45% of the time at starting prices of up to 13/2! The system is highly selective but bets are well worth waiting for and can earn a return on investment figure of around 70% with minimal losing runs.

System Rules

1. Consider All-Weather Flat racing at Lingfield, Southwell and Wolverhampton tracks but do <u>not</u> bet on races for amateur riders.

2. The horse must be top-rated by TOPSPEED in the Racing Post.

3. The horse must be the FORECAST FAVOURITE.

4. The forecast price should be 6/4 to 7/2 inclusive.

5. The horse must be 2 to 5 years of age inclusive.

6. The horse's last run should have been within 31 days.

7. On that occasion it should <u>not</u> have won or finished second.

Results over 3 seasons show an average strike rate of 45% and good level stake profits from surprisingly good prices.

All-Weather Good Things' System Logic

Horses top-rated by Topspeed are always worth consideration, particularly in All-Weather races that are often more 'truly-run' compared to the turf. If the horse is a younger animal, fit from a recent run, and is quoted as the favourite in today's race we are looking at an obvious contender. We want to see the horse ridden by a professional jockey because experience is essential, especially on the All-Weather tracks, so we avoid races for amateur riders.

The proviso that the horse should not have won or placed second last time may seem to fly in the face of punting logic. However, it does make sense. Only a relatively small percentage of Flat horses are consistent enough to record consecutive wins. The fact that our selection may have finished down the field last time doesn't alter the fact that it looks like the best horse today based on its speed figures and its market position. Also, because the majority of punters are strongly influenced by good recent form it is likely that our selection will not be over-backed, thus ensuring a decent price.

All-Weather Good Things System Results

2001 - 17 wins from 41 bets = 41.46% strike rate. Level Stake Profit = 22.05 points. Return on Investment = 53.78%.

2002 - 14 wins from 27 bets = 51.85% strike rate. Level Stake Profit = 23.51 points. Return on Investment = 87.07%.

2003 - 15 wins from 34 bets = 44.12% strike rate. Level Stake Profit = 26.46 points. Return on Investment = 77.82%.

3 years total - 46 wins from 102 bets = 45.10% strike rate.
LSP = 72.02 points. ROI = 70.61%.
Longest winning run 4. Longest losing run 6.
Average winning starting price 11/4.

SECOND SHOT
Flat Racing System

~Profit From Backing Beaten Favourites~

A horse that lost its last race as the favourite but runs again as the market leader can be a good betting proposition, under certain circumstances.

System Rules

1. Consider all flat racing in the UK but for best results only bet during the period April to September inclusive.

2. The horse should be no more than 5 years old.

3. The horse should be the FAVOURITE in the Racing Post betting forecast quoted between 6/4 & 7/2 inclusive.

4. The horse should have started as favourite in its last race.

5. The horse should have LOST its last race. (Next to the horse's name the letters **BF** denote beaten favourite).

6. Today's race should have between 5 & 16 runners inclusive.

7. Consider any type of race except claiming, selling or auction.

8. Do NOT bet odds-on.

A strike rate of over 35% can be expected from an average of one or two bets a day during the main season, with an overall return on investment of around 20%. Verified results for five years are included.

Second Shot Flat System Logic

A horse that lost its last race as the favourite was an obvious disappointment to connections and they will be keen to recoup losses. If the horse has been placed in a race today where it is once again considered to be the market leader there is a good chance of making amends.

It was found that the main turf Flat season was more profitable than All-Weather winter racing. Also claimers and sellers did not yield good results. Concentrating on younger horses (up to five years of age) in fields no bigger than sixteen runners also cut out a lot of losing bets.

Second Shot System Results

1999 - 80 wins from 219 bets = 36.53% strike rate. Level Stake profit = 59.56 points. Return on Investment = 27.20%.

2000 - 72 wins from 197 bets = 35.55% strike rate. Level Stake Profit = 36.98 points. Return on Investment = 18.77%.

2001 - 54 wins from 173 bets = 31.21% strike rate. Level Stake Profit = 10.47 points. Return on Investment = 6.05%.

2002 - 85 wins from 216 bets = 39.35% strike rate. Level Stake Profit = 74.09 points. Return on Investment = 34.30%.

2003 - 82 wins from 248 bets = 33.06% strike rate. Level Stake Profit = 27.97 points. Return on Investment = 11.28%.

5 years total - 373 wins from 1053 bets = 35.42% strike rate.
LSP = 209.07 points. ROI = 19.85%.
Longest winning run 5. Longest losing run 16.
Average winning starting price 5/2.

SECOND SHOT
National Hunt Racing System

~Profit From Backing Beaten Favourites~

A horse that lost its last race as the favourite but runs again as the market leader can be a good betting proposition, under certain circumstances.

System Rules

1. Consider all jump racing in the UK. But for best results only bet during the period October to March inclusive.

2. The horse should be the clear favourite in the Racing Post betting forecast quoted no bigger than 7/2.

3. The horse should have started as favourite in its last race but LOST. (Next to the horse's name on the race card the letters **BF** denote beaten favourite).

4. We only bet in <u>non-handicap races</u> described as Novice Hurdles, Novice Chases or Hunter Chases. The race should not be described as a Seller or Claimer.

Results recorded over four years show a remarkably consistent average strike rate of 55%. Good profits were achieved from an average return of over 23%. As with all high strike rate methods, a sensible staking plan could enhance profits.

Second Shot (NH) System Logic

Exactly the same principle contained in the Flat version of the system applies here.

Once again it was found that the main season (from October to March) was the best time and by far the best strike rate was achieved by concentrating on non-handicap races for Novices or Hunters.

We want to see a clear, strong favourite so we draw the line at a maximum of 7/2 in the forecast.

Second Shot (NH) System Results

1999/2000 - 56 wins from 86 bets = 65.12% strike rate. Level Stake Profit = 26.03 points. Return on Investment = 30.27%.

2000/2001 - 32 wins from 66 bets = 48.48% strike rate. Level Stake Profit = 7.09 points. Return on Investment = 10.74%.

2001/2002 - 53 wins from 102 bets = 51.96% strike rate. Level Stake Profit = 20.81 points. Return on Investment = 20.40%.

2002/2003 - 43 wins from 80 bets = 53.75% strike rate. Level Stake Profit = 24.06 points. Return on Investment = 30.07%.

4 years total - 184 wins from 334 bets = 55.09% strike rate.
LSP = 77.99 points. ROI = 23.35%.
Longest winning run 12. Longest losing run 8.
Average winning starting price 5/4.

FALLON'S FLYERS
Racing System

Following top jockey Kieren Fallon can be very profitable especially when he does not ride the favourite.

System Rules

1. Consider all horses ridden by K. Fallon (on turf or All-Weather).

2. The horse's last run must have been seven days ago or less.

3. The horse should be two to seven years old inclusive.

4. The horse should be quoted as the second, third or fourth favourite in the Racing Post betting forecast.

Results over six years show a consistent average strike rate of 31%. Around thirty bets a year yield excellent profits and return on investment. Note that there were very few runs during 2000 due to Kieren's injuries sidelining him for most of the season.

Fallon's Flyers System Logic

It's never a bad idea to give close consideration to any horse ridden by the champion jockey but you would be hard pressed to make a profit backing favourites as these are often over-bet to very short odds. However, if we turn our attention to the lesser market leaders we find that a very handsome profit can be made from the better prices, particularly if we concentrate on younger fit horses running within seven days of their last outing.

This system has found some big winning starting prices up to 20/1.

Fallon's Flyers System Results

1998 - 9 wins from 23 bets = 39.13% strike rate.
Level Stake Profit = 27.50 points. Return on Investment = 119.57%.

1999 - 11 wins from 38 bets = 28.95% strike rate.
Level Stake Profit = 36.13 points. Return on Investment = 95.08%.

2000 - 3 wins from 9 bets = 33.33% strike rate.
Level Stake Profit = 3.25 points. Return on Investment = 36.11%

2001 - 10 wins from 29 bets = 34.48 strike rate.
Level Stake Profit = 24.50 points. Return on Investment = 84.48%.

2002 - 7 wins from 25 bets = 28% strike rate.
Level Stake Profit = 7.75 points. Return on Investment = 31%.

2003 - 8 wins from 31 bets = 25.81% strike rate.
Level Stake Profit = 22.63 points. Return on Investment = 73%.

6 years total - 48 wins from 155 bets = 30.97% strike rate.
LSP = 121.76 points. ROI = 78.55%.
Longest winning run 4. Longest losing run 8.
Average winning starting price 5/1.

THE CHESTER RACING SYSTEM

The low draw bias at Chester's tight turning track is well known. Blindly backing the draw, over the last four years, has shown good profits from some big priced winners.

This is our very simple system.

1. **At Chester back all horses drawn in the lowest quintile.** (This means we divide the field into five parts and back the lowest part. In other words, in a five-runner field we would only back stall 1. In a race with six to ten runners we would back stalls 1 & 2. Eleven to fifteen runners would mean three bets on stalls 1, 2 & 3. Sixteen to twenty runners would require four bets.

2. We cover all races at Chester but, for best results, ensure there is a <u>minimum of five runners</u>. Also, leave out any marathon races (such as The Chester Cup) and draw the line at a maximum of one mile six furlongs.

We do not expect a high strike rate with such a method but the published results over four years reveal exciting betting opportunities.

A). The system will often throw up BIG priced selections so place betting is always an option. Each-way doubles and Tote Placepot perms can be very rewarding.

B). On several occasions the system has found the first and second horse and, occasionally, even the third as well. This means some BIG payouts are possible betting on Forecasts and Tricasts.

The Chester Racing System's Recent Results

A great start to the season at the 2004 May Meeting.

5th May

1:55pm DANCE NIGHT **Won 15/8** SAPPHIRE DREAM 2nd 8/1 **(Forecast £17.63)**

2:25pm HIDDEN HOPE **Won 14/1** MENHOUBAH 2nd 7/1 **(Forecast £99-61)**

3:30pm LAKE GARDA **Won 8/1** BENBAUN Lost INSTANT RECALL Lost

4:05pm THE TERMINATOR Lost VICTORIA PEEK Lost

4:40pm HARRY UP Lost SIR ERNEST Lost DEMOLITION MOLLY Lost

5:15pm PIPER LILY Lost

6th May

1:55pm ASIATIC 2nd 5/1 MARINE CITY Lost

2:25pm OASIS STAR **Won 5/1** GLARAMARA 3rd 8/1 SKYHARBOR Lost CELLO Lost

2:55pm GRAHAM ISLAND Lost TEMPLE PLACE Lost

3:30pm PARASOL 2nd 2/1 HAMBLEDEN Lost

4:05pm PETRULA 2nd 7/1 CROW WOOD 3rd 10/1 FISIO THERAPY Lost

4:40pm NOORA 2nd 7/2

7th May

1:55pm SIMIANNA 2nd 8/1 MAKTAVISH 3rd 7/2

2:55pm COMPTON BOLTER 3rd 15/2 RAWYAAN Lost

3:30pm LINE DRAWING 2nd 9/2 LARKWING 3rd 5/4

4:05pm CHAPPEL CRESENT **Won 15/2** NASHAAB 2nd 5/1 RETIREMENT 3rd 2/1
        H HARRISON Lost **(Forecast £42-10 Tricast £108-78)**

4:40pm MR LEAR Lost CHAMPION LION Lost BAKIRI Lost

<u>The Chester Racing System Logic</u>

This system has no logic other than the draw at Chester that has such a strong bias you can literally back it blindly. It is probably the closest I get to a true 'gambling' system where all the usual criteria are thrown completely out of the window! I can never resist it however and use it to small stakes with the Tote betting on Placepots, Forecasts and Tricasts. It's a lot of fun and occasionally pays out big time. It has actually found winners up to 66/1!

Chester Racing System Results

2000 - 22 wins from 92 bets = 23.91% strike rate.
Level Stake Profit = 11.69 points. Return on Investment = 11.69%.

2001 - 14 wins from 100 bets = 14% strike rate.
Level Stake Profit = 55.23 points. Return on Investment = 55.23%.

2002 - 16 wins from 97 bets = 16.49% strike rate.
Level Stake Profit = 8.76 points. Return on Investment = 9.03%.

2003 - 18 wins from 101 bets = 17.82% strike rate.
Level Stake Profit = 65.69 points. Return on Investment = 65.04%.

4 years total - 70 wins from 390 bets = 17.95% strike rate.
LSP = 141.37 points. ROI = 36.25%.
Longest winning run 3. Longest losing run 15.
Average winning starting price 13/2.

Thank you for buying and reading this book. I sincerely hope it helps in your quest for winners. Please contact me if I can send you details of my latest published systems:

Bernard Hibbert
CHESTER RACING CLUB
Chantry Court
Chester
CH1 4QN
bernard@chesterracingclub.com

Website www.chesterracingclub.com

This book is published by

SPORTSWORLD PUBLISHING Ltd.
Raines House,
Denby Dale Road,
Wakefield
WF1 1HL
E-mail: customercare@sportsworldpublishing.co.uk

RACING INVESTORS CLUB

Bernard Hibbert is a regular contributor to the Racing Investors Club. The club was founded in January 2006 by a small group of dedicated professionals with one aim in mind – to make a serious income from Horse Racing.

The Racing Investors Club brings together a small team of racing experts, systems analysts and professional punters. It is their aim to collaborate with members to create an investment approach to our betting so that we can all benefit from consistent profits.

One of the main features of our club is the monthly report posted to all members featuring racing methods and ideas that have been **tried and tested** over lengthy periods. Advice on system operation, staking plans and other betting strategies will be discussed in detail and all members are encouraged to participate with their own ideas and contributions via the Members Forum. We feel that this is the best racing forum available – why not try it?

For more information please contact club secretary, Don Hydes on 0871 871 9877 or email him at customercare@sportsworldpublishing.co.uk. Alternatively visit

www.sportsworldpublishing.co.uk